More of the
World's Best
Dirty Limericks

In this series

Richard O'Toole

More of the World's Best Dirty Limericks

Cartoons by Graham Morris

HarperCollins*Publishers*

HarperCollins*Publishers*
77–85 Fulham Palace Road
Hammersmith, London W6 8JB

A Paperback Original 1994
1 3 5 7 9 8 6 4 2

A catalogue record for this book
is available from the British Library

ISBN 0 00 638374 2

Set in Linotron Goudy Old Style by
Rowland Phototypesetting Ltd, Bury St Edmunds, Suffolk

Printed in Great Britain by
HarperCollinsManufacturing Glasgow

The limerick is furtive and mean,
You must keep her in close quarantine,
Or she sneaks to the slums
And promptly becomes
Disorderly, drunk and obscene.

The limerick is callous and crude,
Its morals distressingly lewd.
It's not worth the reading
By persons of breeding,
It's designed for us vulgar and rude.

It needn't have ribaldry's taint,
Or strive to make readers feel faint.
There's a type that's demure,
And perfectly pure,
But it helps quite a lot if it ain't.

There was a young girl of Bermuda
Who shot a nocturnal intruder.
　　It was not her ire,
　　At her lack of attire.
But his grabbing her jewels while he screwed her.

There was a young fellow named Boeing,
Whose penis kept growing and growing.
　　It grew so tremendous,
　　So gross and horrendous,
'Twas no good for f*****g, just showing.

A Salvation lassie named Claire,
Was having her first love affair.
　　As she climbed into bed,
　　She reverently said,
'I wish to be opened with prayer.'

There was a young fellow named Baker
  Who screwed a vivacious young Quaker,
      And when he had done it,
      She straightened her bonnet,
And said, 'I give thanks to my Maker.'

There was a young sailor from Brighton
  Who said to a girl, 'You're a tight one.'
      She replied, ''Pon my soul,
      You're in the wrong hole,
There's plenty of room in the right one.'

There was a young lady of Exeter
  Who found that her boyfriend was vexed at her.
      But she thought he went far
      When he waved from his car
The distinguishing mark of his sex at her.

It always delights me at Hanks
To walk up the old river banks.
    One time in the grass,
    I stepped on an arse,
And heard a young girl murmur, 'Thanks.'

A fellow whose surname was Hunt
Trained his tool to perform a slick stunt.
    This versatile spout
    Could be turned inside out,
Like a glove, and be used as a cunt.

There was a young man of Bengal
Who went to a fancy-dress ball
    Arrayed like a tree,
    But he failed to foresee
His abuse by the dogs in the hall.

A copper of Nottingham Junction,
  Whose organ had long ceased to function,
        Deceived his good wife
        For the rest of her life
With the aid of his constable's truncheon.

There was a young lady named Gloria
  Who was had by Sir Roger de Maurier,
        Six other men,
        Sir Roger again,
And the band at the Waldorf Astoria.

There was a young lady of Pecking
  Who indulged in a great deal of necking.
        This seemed a great waste,
        Since she claimed to be chaste –
This statement, however, needs checking.

Kind Sir, my name it is Mabel,
And though I don't know if I'm able,
    I am willing to try,
    So where shall I lie,
On the bed, or the floor, or the table?

A lassie from wee Ballachulish
Observed, 'Och, virginity's foolish.
    When a lad makes a try,
    To say ought but "Aye"
Would be stubborn, pig-headed and foolish.'

There was a young lady of Devon
Who was screwed in the garden by seven
    High Anglican priests,
    The lascivious beasts.
Of such is the Kingdom of Heaven.

There was a young maiden of Gloucester,
  Whose parents thought they had lost her,
      Till they found in the grass
      The print of her arse,
And the knees of the man who had crossed her.

There was a young girl from Hoboken
  Who claimed that her hymen was broken
      From riding a bike
      On a cobblestone pike,
But really 'twas broken from pokin'.

God's plan made a hopeful beginning,
  But man spoiled his chances by sinning.
      We trust that the story
      Will end in God's glory,
But at present the other side's winning.

A maiden attending Bryn Mawr
Committed a dreadful *faux pas*.
    She loosened a stay,
    In her *décolleté*,
Exposing her *je ne sais quoi*.

A churchman austere and refined,
Caught with hand on a lady's behind,
    Cried, 'Our ministry's such
    That we must keep in touch
With the widely felt needs of mankind.'

A churchman austere and refined
Said, 'This age most permissive I find,
    But nude shows on TV
    Do not upset me,
It's the staying up late that I mind.'

A churchman austere and refined,
To a celibate life was resigned,
    Till he studied the laws
    And discovered the flaws,
Then a lady friend made up his mind.

A pretty young lady named Flo,
Said, 'I hate to be had in the snow.
    While I'm normally hot,
    In this spot I am not,
So as soon as you come, Bert, let's go.'

The late Brigham Young was no neuter,
No faggot, no fairy, no fruiter.
    Where ten thousand virgins
    Succumbed to his urgin's
There now stands the great state of Utah.

There was a young laundress named Wrangle
Whose tits tilted up at an angle.
    'They may tickle my chin,'
    She said with a grin,
'But at least they keep out of the mangle.'

A complacent old don of Divinity,
Used to boast of his daughters' virginity.
    They must have been dawdlin',
    Down at old Magdalen,
It wouldn't have happened at Trinity.

An innocent virgin of Clewer,
Incited her boyfriend to screw her.
    She tried to say no,
    A half-second slow,
Now when she sits down she says 'Oo-er'.

There was a young lady from Thrace,
　Whose corset got too tight to lace.
　　　Her mother said, 'Nelly,
　　　There's more in your belly,
Than ever went in through your face.'

There was a young lady named Mabel
　Who used to sprawl out on the table,
　　　Then cry to her man,
　　　'Get in all you can,
Get your balls in as well, if you're able.'

There was a young lady named Hitchin
　Who was scratching her cunt in the kitchen.
　　　Her mother said, 'Rose,
　　　It's the crabs, I suppose.'
She said, 'Yes, and the buggers are itchin'.'

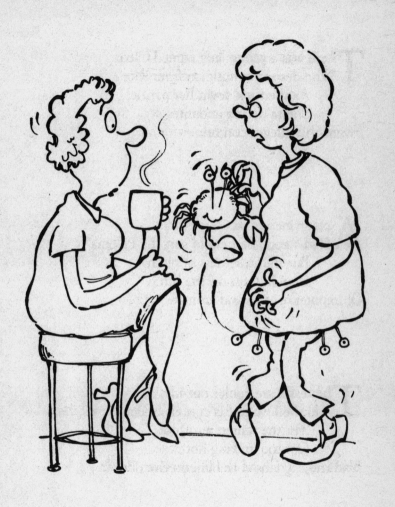

There was a young lady named Cleo
Who desired a musician from Rio.
    As she took down her panties,
    She said, 'No andantes,
I want this allegro con brio.'

A clergyman from Oklahoma
Had a cock that could sing 'La Paloma',
    But the sweetness of pitch
    Couldn't put off the hitch
Of impotence, size and aroma.

'The testes are cooler outside,'
said the Doc to his curious bride,
    'For the semen must not
    Get too fucking hot,
And the bag fans your bum on the ride.'

There was a young lady named Bradley
  Who slept with a man who fucked madly.
        He gave her the crabs,
        And the numerous scabs,
And the pox, too, she got very badly.

There was a young fellow named Willie
  Who acted remarkably silly.
        At the All-Nations Ball,
        Dressed in nothing at all,
He claimed that his costume was chilly.

A parson who lived in King's Lynn
  Said he thought fornication was sin,
        Till a girl said 'You fool,'
        Went and took out his tool,
Took her drawers off and shoved it right in.

An accident really uncanny
Befell a young lady named Annie.
    She sat on a chair,
    When her false teeth were there,
And bit herself, right on the fanny.

There was a young girl of Kilkenny
On whose genital parts there were many
    Venereal growths,
    The result of wild oats,
Sown there by a fellow named Benny.

There was a young fellow from Parma
Who was screwing a young maiden, a charmer.
    Said the damsel demure,
    'You'll excuse me I'm sure,
But I must say you fuck like a farmer.'

There was a young Bishop from Brest,
Who openly practised incest.
    'My sisters and nieces
    Are all dandy pieces,
And they don't cost a cent,' he confessed.

There was a young parson named Lynn,
Whose cock was the size of a pin.
    Said his girl with a laugh,
    As she handled his staff,
'Well, this won't be much of a sin.'

Said a certain old Earl that I knew,
'I've been struck from the rolls of *Who's Who*,
    Just because I was found
    Lying flat on the ground
With the housemaid – and very nice too.'

When a certain young curate in Leeds
  Was discovered one day in the weeds
      Astride a young nun,
      He said, 'This is fun,
Much better than telling one's beads.'

There was a French painter, Matisse,
  Who said as he tumbled his niece,
      'You claim it feels awful,
      And I know 'tis unlawful,'
Then his parrot called in the police.

An artist called Sammy McHugh
  Once painted his organ dark blue.
      When he'd finished his work
      He remarked, with a smirk,
'Now I've got a reply for "What's new?"'

A willing young girl named Cervantes
Cried, 'Sure you can feel in my panties!
    I'd of course draw the line
    If the panties were mine,
But these aren't my panties, they're Aunty's.'

She entertained men of all nations,
Causing various and lustful sensations.
    When asked, 'Are those dozens
    Of callers your cousins?'
She said, 'No, just sexual relations.'

A young maid by name Gambietta
Once used an imperfect French letter.
    This was not the worst,
    With the pox she got cursed,
And she took a long time to get better.

In a laundrette, waiting to rinse,
An innocent fellow named Vince
    Saw lovely Miss Hyer
    Put her drawers in the dryer –
He hasn't been quite the same since.

'At last I've seduced the au pair
With some steak and a chocolate éclair,
    Some peas and some chips,
    Three Walnut Whips,
And a carafe of *vin ordinaire*.'

Charlotte Brontë said, 'Sister, oh what a man,
He laid me face down on the ottoman.
    Now don't you and Emily
    Go telling the family,
But he smacked me upon my bare bottom, Anne.'

There was a young fellow of Wadham
Who asked for a ticket to Sodom.
　　　When they said, 'We prefer
　　　Not to issue them, Sir,'
He said, 'Don't call me Sir, call me Modom.'

A pretty young lady named Claire
Remarked as she sprawled in a chair,
　　　'I can see by your glance
　　　I forgot to wear pants,
So stare at me bare, I don't care.'

A Turk found a Greek in his harem,
And snarled, 'You bastard, you'll scare 'em.
　　　I'm calling my wranglers
　　　To cut off your danglers,
From now on you ain't gonna wear 'em.'

A newly-wed charmer of Wheeling
Sighed, 'A honeymoon seemed so appealing,
　　But for more than two weeks
　　All I've heard are bed squeaks,
And all that I've seen is the ceiling.'

His model cried to Botticelli
As he bounced up and down on her belly,
　　'While you're driving me wild
　　Please recall I'm with child,
And you're beating the brat to a jelly.'

A professor at Oxford named Wilde
By the sweet smell of sex was beguiled.
　　Losing all moral scruples
　　He raped forty pupils,
And got thirty-seven with child.

A maidenhead hunter named Drew,
Whose morals were terribly few,
    Said, 'At first some will balk,
    But gin and sweet talk
Makes 'em do what they said they won't do.'

A pretty young lady from Gloucester
Met a passionate fellow who tossed her.
    She wasn't much hurt,
    But he dirtied her skirt –
Oh! Think of the anguish it cost her.

There was a young lady named Sue
Who preferred a stiff drink to a screw,
    But one leads to the other
    And now she's a mother,
Let this be a lesson to you.

A worried young man from Stamboul
Discovered red rings on his tool.
    Said the doctor, a cynic,
    'Get out of my clinic,
Just wipe off the lipstick, you fool.'

A bibulous bishop would preach
After sunning his balls on the beach,
    But his love life was ended
    By a paunch so distended
It annulled, *ipso facto*, his reach.

A cute debutante from St Paul
Wore a newspaper dress to a ball.
    The dress caught on fire,
    And burnt her entire
Front page, sporting section and all.

When a young girl got married in Bicester
Her mother remarked as she kissed her,
    'That fellow you've won
    Is sure to be fun,
Since tea he's fucked me and your sister.'

There was a young maid of Siam
Who said to her lover, Kiam,
    'If you kiss me of course
    You will have to use force,
Thank God you are stronger than I am.'

There was a young lady of Kent
Who said that she knew what it meant
    When men asked her to dine
    Upon lobster and wine.
She knew, oh she knew, but she went.

There was a young actress from Kew
  Who said as the bishop withdrew,
      'The vicar is quicker
      And slicker and thicker,
And three inches longer than you.'

There was a young maiden from Tyre
  Who succumbed to her lover's desire.
      She said, 'It's a sin,
      But now that it's in,
Could you shove it a few inches higher?'

There was a young girl of Decatur
  Who went out to sea on a freighter.
      She was screwed by the master –
      An utter disaster –
But the crew all made up for it later.

Astableman fresh from the Ruhr
Had a daughter delightful and pure.
    It seems such a shame
    That her chief claim to fame
Was her great skill at pitching manure.

There was a crusader of Parma
Who went to bed with his charma;
    She, naturally nude,
    Said: 'Don't think me rude,
But do you think you should take off your arma?'

A colonial girl sweet and sainted
Was by war-striped young Indians tainted.
    When asked of the ravages
    She said of the savages,
'They aren't half as bad as they're painted.'

At a bullfight, José made his bid.
When the maiden agreed, he was rid
　　　Of all inhibitions, and
　　　Despite the conditions,
As the crowd yelled 'Olé!', José did.

A certain young girl from Key West
Was unusually large in the chest.
　　　Her boyfriend's attention
　　　To her outside dimension
Brought his own measurement to its best.

In the soap operas seen in Gomorrah
The heroine wakes up in horror
　　　To find a huge prick,
　　　Nearly three inches thick
Half-way up her – please tune in tomorrow.

The bishop of Tessofarnonga
Could stand his seclusion no longer.
    His habits monastic
    Were very elastic,
But, unhappily, so was his donga.

The bishop of the Ibu plantation
Wrote a thesis on configuration
    For the *Christian Review*,
    As all bishops do,
Whilst practising miscegenation.

The charm of a whore in Shalott
Was the absence of hair on her twat.
    She kept it smooth looking
    Not by shaving or plucking
But by all of the fucking she got.

The rosy-cheeked lass from Dunellen,
Who the Hoboken sailors call Helen,
  In her efforts to please
  Spreads social disease
From New York to the Straits of Magellan.

There was a young girl of Mauritius
Who said, 'John, that fuck was delicious.
  But the next time you come,
  Won't you come up my bum,
That wart on your cock looks suspicious.'

There was a young lady named Alice,
Who purchased a hard rubber phallus.
  Since she learned its perfections,
  She hates doctors' inspections –
It's such an odd place for a callus.

There was a young lady named Shriver
  Who was screwed in the ass by a driver,
      And when she complained
      He said, 'Sorry you're pained,'
And gave her a fiver to bribe her.

There was a young lady of Joppa
  Who came a society cropper.
      She went to Ostend
      With a gentleman friend,
And the rest of the story's improper.

There was a young fellow named Treet
  Who minced as he walked down the street.
      He wore shoes of bright red,
      And playfully said,
'I may not be throng but I'm thweet.'

An erotic neurotic named Syd
Got his Ego confused with his Id.
    His libido was channelized
    So he got psychoanalyzed,
And that's why he done what he did.

When the judge with his wife having sport
Proved suddenly two inches short,
    The good woman declined
    And the judge had her fined,
By proving contempt of the court.

Said a certain young red-headed siren,
'Young sailors are cute, I must try one.'
    She came home in the nude,
    Starved, screwed and tattooed
With lewd pictures and verses by Byron.

A widow who lived in Rangoon
Hung a black-ribboned wreath near her womb.
    'To remind me,' she said,
    'Of my husband, who's dead,
And of what put him into his tomb.'

A pretty young girl of Peru
Had nothing whatever to do
    But sit on the stairs,
    And count her cunt hairs –
Four thousand, three hundred and two.

On May Day the girls of Penzance,
Being bored by a lack of romance,
    Joined the workers' parade
    With this banner displayed,
'What the pants of Penzance needs is ants.'

As we went in the lift from floor four
Poor Sue caught her tits in the door.
        She yelled a good deal,
        But had they been real,
She'd have yelled out a bloody sight more.

The last time I dined with the King
He did a most curious thing.
        He sat on a stool
        And took out his tool,
And said, 'If I play, will you sing?'

There is a young nurse in Japan
Who lifts men by their pricks to the pan,
        A trick of ju-jitsu,
        And either it shits you,
Or makes you feel more of a man.

There was a young cowboy named Garry
  Who was morbidly anxious to marry,
      But he found the defection
      Of any erection
A difficult factor to parry.

There was an old countess of Bray,
  And you may think it odd when I say,
      Notwithstanding her station,
      And high education,
She always spelt cunt with a K.

There was a young man from Liberia
  Who was feeling a wench from Nigeria.
      He said, 'Say, my pet,
      Your panties are wet.'
'Sorry, sir, but that's my interior.'

When the Bermondsey Bricklayers struck,
  Bill Bloggins was having a fuck.
      By union rules
      He had to down tools,
Now wasn't that bloody bad luck.

A nudist by name Roger Peet
 Loved to dance in the snow and the sleet,
      But one chilly December
      He froze every member,
And retired to a monkish retreat.

There was a young maiden of Natchez
 Who fell in some nettle wood patches.
      She sits in her room
      With her bare little moon,
And scratches and scratches and scratches.

All winter the Eunuch from Munich
  Went walking in naught but his tunic.
     Folks said, 'You've a cough,
     And you'll freeze your balls off.'
Said he, 'That is why I'm a Eunuch.'

Growing tired of her husband's great mass,
  A young bride inserted some glass.
     The prick of her hubby
     Is now short and stubby,
While the wife now can piss through her ass.

There was a young lady named Dowd
  Whom a bold fellow groped in the crowd.
     But the thing that most vexed her
     Was that when he stood next her
He said, 'How's your cunt?' right out loud.

There was a young girl from the Creek
Had her periods twice every week.
  Said the Vicar from Woking,
  'How very provoking,
There's no time for sex, so to speak.'

There was a young girl in a cast
Who had an unsavoury past,
  For the neighbourhood pastor
  Tried fucking through plaster,
And his very first fuck was his last.

There was an old man of Malucca
Who went to his daughter to spank her,
  But she got the best
  Of his little incest,
And gave the old fucker the chancre.

A clever young doctor of Chester
Has a new electronic cunt tester.
    With an LED eye,
    A drill and a die,
It inspects every pimple and fester.

A young girl who was no good at tennis,
But at swimming was really a menace,
    Took pains to explain,
    'It depends how you train –
I was a street walker in Venice.'

There was a young girl of St Cyr
Whose reflex reactions were queer.
    Her escort said, 'Mabel,
    Please get off the table,
That money's to pay for the beer.'

A sailor, ashore in Peru,
Said, '*Signora, quanto por la screw?*'
    'For only one peso
    I will, if you say so,
Be buggered and nibble it too.'

A weary young maiden of Nome
Was worn out from inviting men home.
    Eight friends came for screwing,
    But she said, 'Nothing doing,
One of you will have to go home.'

There was a young maid named McGee
Who was always in form for a spree.
    She said 'For a buck,
    I will give you a fuck,
And I'll throw in the ass hole for free.'

The enjoyment of sex, although great,
Is in later years said to abate.
This well may be so,
But what would I know?
I'm now only seventy-eight.

There was a young girl from Madrid
Who her friends used to fuck for a quid.
But a rotten Italian,
With balls like a stallion,
Said he'd do it for free – And he did.

There was a young maiden of Chester
Who said to the man that undressed her,
'I think you will find
That it's better behind,
The front is beginning to fester.'

A skinny young maid of Verdun
Wed a big German's poor endowed son.
    She said, 'I don't care,
    If there isn't much there,
God knows it is better than none.'

There was a young fellow named Oudh
Whose mind was exceedingly lewd.
    He asserted, 'All women
    Seen dancin' or swimmin',
Would be better off home getting screwed.'

A lisping young lady named Beth
Was saved from a fate worse than death
    Seven times in a row,
    Which unsettled her so
That she quit saying 'No' and said 'Yeth'.

There was a young maid of New York
Who plugged up her cunt with a cork,
But being quite lewd
She asked to be screwed
In the ass by her friend, Johnny Warke.

There was a young virgin of Bude
Whose tricks, though exciting, were viewed
With distrust by the men,
For she'd feel them and then,
When they wanted to fuck her, she sued.

The typists at Wheesly and Beesly
All fornicate keenly and easily.
In this pleasant way,
They add to their pay,
Which at Wheesly and Beesly is measly.

I once had the wife of a Dean
Seven times when the Dean was gone ski'in'.
      She remarked with some gaiety,
      'Not bad for the laity,
But the Bishop once managed thirteen.'

There was a young lady named Bickers
   Whose cousin came off in her knickers,
      But a sperm out in front
      Found its way to her cunt,
So then they went round to the vicar's.

A schoolgirl who reached adolescence
  Asked, what did they mean by pubescence?
      Said the vicar, 'A dame
      And a man ain't the same,'
And he widened her slit with the difference.

Said a crafty old doctor named Sammon,
'Impotence is getting too common.
     Pills, oysters and honey
     Are sheer waste of money,
What works is to bed a fresh woman.'

An actor in furious rage
   Muttered this to an actress on stage –
     'When I'd fallen for you,
     I had thought forty-two
Was meant for your tits not your age.'

There was a young girl named Lorraine
   Whom no one could think of as plain.
     The fellows pursued her
     In order to screw her,
Again and again and again.

An insatiable damsel named Bridget
Was likely to mutter and fidget
    Whenever some pup
    Couldn't seem to work up
A quick enough rise to the rigid.

A seductive Dolores could lay so
That she earned herself many a peso,
    From men who walked miles
    To climax with smiles.
(Her ads in the papers all say so.)

Softly seductive young Brenda
Wants a man who is sweet, kind and tender,
    And thoughtful and bright,
    And sexually right,
But mostly a very big spender.

There was a young lady named Flynn
Who thought fornication was sin,
But when she was tight
She thought 'twas all right,
So everyone filled her with gin.

A homo who lived in Macroom
Took a lesbian up to his room.
They argued all night
About who had the right
To do what, with which and to whom.

The Venerable Lord Bishop of Buckingham,
Stood in front of the manse at old Rockingham.
He was watching the stunts
Of the cunts in the punts,
And the tricks of the pricks who were fucking 'em.

There was an old fellow of Cosham
Who took out his bollocks to wash 'em.
His wife said, 'Oh, Jack!
If you don't put them back,
I will jump on the darn things and squash 'em.'

A young fencing master named Fisk,
As he moved was exceedingly brisk.
When he was in action
The Lorenz contraction
Foreshortened his cock to a disc.

There was a GI name of Snyder
Who took a girl out just to ride her.
She allowed him to feel
From her arse to her heel,
But just would not let him inside her.

The conductor with voice like a hatchet
Observed to a cellist from Datchet,
    'You have twixt your thighs,
    My dear, a great prize –
And yet you just sit there and scratch it.'

A lecherous student from Leeds
One day had to pay for his deeds
    When a man with a gun
    Said, 'You'll marry her, son,
You must harvest when you sow the seeds.'

To his wife said Sir Hubert De Dawes,
'Fix this chastity belt 'neath your drawers.'
    But an amorous Celt
    Found the key to the belt
While the Squire was away at the wars.

There was a poor friar named Tuck,
  Whose sex life was marred by ill luck.
      His physique grew so fat
      That he could not get at
His dong when he wanted to fuck.

When a young girl got married in Chester,
  Her mother she kissed and blessed her.
      She said, 'You're in luck,
      He's a very good fuck.
I had him myself once, in Leicester.'

A pretty wench from Aberystwyth
Took grain to the mill to be grist with.
      The miller's son Jack
      Laid her flat on her back
And united the parts that they pissed with.

There was a young man of Bengal
Who went to a fancy-dress ball,
    And just for a stunt
    He dressed as a cunt,
And was had by a dog in the hall.

There was a young man of Siberia
Whose morals were grossly inferior.
    He slept with a nun,
    Which he shouldn't have done,
And now she's a Mother Superior.

There was a young lady named Smale
Who offered her body for sale.
    To be kind to the blind
    She embossed her behind
With detailed instructions in Braille.

There was a young student of Trinity
Who took his young sister's virginity.
    He buggered his brother,
    Gave twins to his mother,
And then took a degree in Divinity.

There was a young lady named Heather
Whose vulva was tough as old leather.
    She made an odd noise
    For attracting the boys
By flapping the edges together.

There was a young fellow, a banker,
Who had bubo, itch, pox and the chancre.
    He picked up all four
    From a pretty young whore,
So he sent her a postcard to thank her.

A señora who strolled on the Corso
Displayed quite a lot of her torso.
    A crowd soon collected
    But no one objected,
Though some were in favour of more so.

There was a young girl from Tralee
Who went to the river to pee.
    A man in a punt
    Put his hand on her cunt –
My word, how I wish it was me.

There was a young girl of Tralee
Whose knowledge of French was 'Oui, oui'.
    When they asked 'Voulez-Vous?'
    She replied 'Up yours too.'
She was known for her bright repartee.

There was a young lady of Slough
Who said that she didn't know hough.
    Then a young fellow caught her
    And jolly well taught her,
And she can't get enough of it nough.

There was a young Spaniard from Sitges
Who kept all the tourists in stitges
    By parading around
    With an ominous frown
And a bulge in the front of his britges.

Said the Venerable Dean of St Pauls,
'Concerning the cracks in the walls.
    Do you think it would do,
    If we filled them with glue?'
But the Bishop of Lincoln said, 'Balls.'

There was a young lady of Clewer
    Who was riding a bike and it threw her.
        A man saw her there,
        With her legs in the air,
And seized the occasion to screw her.

The new cinematic emporium
    Is not just a super-sensorium,
        But a highly effectual
        Heterosexual
Mutual masturbatorium.

Consistent disciples of Marx
    Will have to employ special narks
        If nationalization
        Of all copulation
Leads to *laissez-faire* fucking in parks.

King Richard, in one of his rages,
Forsook his good lady for ages,
    And rested in bed
    With a good book instead,
Or, preferably, one of the pages.

There once was a monarch called Harry
Whose efforts seemed doomed to miscarry,
    Since his wish for a son,
    Plus unlimited fun,
Made him marry and marry and marry.

King Henry the Eighth was a Tudor,
Of our monarchs we've witnessed few ludor;
    Each wife that he wed,
    He led to the bed,
Where he vudor and wudor and scrudor.

Said the famous philosopher, Russell:
'One can come without moving a muscle.
    When sufficiently blotto,
    Just watch Lady Otto-
line's bum as it bursts from her bustle.'

The last time I slept with the Queen
She said, as I whistled 'Ich Dien':
    'It's royalty's night out,
    But please put the light out,
The Queen may be had, but not seen.'

A divine by the name of McWhinners
Held classes each evening for sinners.
    They were sectioned and graded
    So the very degraded
Would not be held back by beginners.

There isn't a shadow of doubt
We're all of us on the way out,
  From old age or ambition
  Or excessive coition –
So drink up before you are nowt.

A young man by a girl was desired
To give her the thrills she required,
  But he died of old age
  Ere his cock could assauge
The volcanic desires it inspired.

There was an old fellow named Hewing
Whose heart stopped while he was a-screwing.
  He gasped: 'Really, Miss,
  Don't feel bad about this –
There's nothing I'd rather die doing.'

If intercourse gives you thrombosis,
And continence causes neurosis,
    I'd rather expire
    Fulfulling desire
Than live in a state of psychosis.

There was a young lady of Cheadle
Who once gave the pox to the beadle.
    When she said, 'Does it itch?'
    He said, 'You young bitch,
It hurts me like hell when I peedle.'

Ascribe, to the vulgar inclined,
Wrote a drama more gross than refined,
    With words, all four-letter,
    Hips, nips, tits and better,
Like those that have just crossed your mind.

Far beyond all the girls of Pirelli
Are the females of S. Botticelli.
    Each has porcelain skin
    And a pert pointed chin,
And erogenous botti and belli.

There was a young man of Ostend
Who went for a drink with a friend.
    They had a few jars
    With two boys in some bars,
And so each had a friend in the end.

'COME TO NOAH's for wine and strong waters,
And for fucking in clean classy quarters.
    I assure every guest
    I've made personal test
Of my booze and my beds and my daughters.'

A lady on climbing Mount Shasta
Complained when the mountain grew vaster.
    It wasn't the climb,
    The dirt or the grime,
But the ice on her ass that harassed her.

There was a young girl of Trebarwith
Whom a cad in a car went too far with,
    Which disproves a report
    That she wasn't the sort
For going too far in a car with.

A girl who was touring Zambesi
Said: 'Attracting the men is quite easy.
    I don't wear any pants,
    And, at every chance,
I stand where it's frightfully breezy.'

There was a young fellow named Chick
 Who fancied himself rather slick.
      He went to a ball,
      Dressed in nothing at all,
But a big velvet bow round his prick.

There was a young maid of Peru
 Who swore that she never would screw,
      Except under stress
      Of forceful duress,
Like: 'I'm ready. So how about you?'

Said the newly-weds staying near Kitely,
 'We turn out the electric light nightly.
      It's best to embark
      Upon sex in the dark,
The look of the thing's so unsightly.'

A business-like harlot named Draper
Once tried an unusual caper.
    What made it so nice
    Was you got it half price
If you brought in her ad from the paper.

Of my husband I do not ask much,
Just an all mod. and con. little hutch,
    Bank account in my name,
    With a cheque book to same,
Plus a small fee for fucking and such.

Up the street sex is sold by the piece,
And I wish that foul traffic would cease.
    It's a shame and improper,
    And I'd phone for a copper,
But that's where you'll find all the police.

There was an old madam called Rainey,
Adept at her business and brainy.
    She charged ten bucks or more
    For a seasoned old whore,
But a dollar would get you a trainee.

When a friend told a typist called Eve,
'Your boss is too good to believe.
    You can't type, you can't spell.
    Why's he pay you so well?'
She answered: 'I cannot conceive.'

It seems I impregnated Marge,
So I do rather feel, by and large,
    Some dough should be tendered
    For services rendered,
But I can't quite decide what to charge.

On an outing with seventeen Czechs
A girl tourist supplied the free sex.
    She returned from the jaunt
    Feeling more or less gaunt,
But the Czechs were all absolute wrecks.

When Daddy and Mummy got plastered,
    And their shame had been thoroughly mastered,
    They told their boy, Harry,
    'Son, we never did marry.
But don't tell the neighbours, you bastard.'

Though his plan, when he gave her a buzz,
    Was to do what man normally does,
    She declared: 'I'm a soul,
    Not a sexual goal' –
So he shrugged, and called someone who was.

Widow (conscious that time's on the wing),
Fortyish, but still game for a fling,
　　Seeks fun-loving male,
　　Mature, but not stale,
With a view to the usual thing.

There was a young fellow named Fife
Whose marriage was ruined for life,
　　For he had an aversion
　　To every perversion,
And only liked screwing his wife.

But one year the poor woman struck,
And she wept and she cursed at her luck:
　　'Oh, where has it gotten us,
　　This goddam monotonous
Fuck after fuck after fuck.'

There once was a floozie named Annie
Whose prices were cosy – but canny.
    A buck for a fuck,
    Fifty cents for a suck,
And a dime for a feel of her fanny.

A shiftless young fellow of Kent
Had his wife fuck the landlord for rent,
    But as she grew older
    The landlord grew colder,
And now they live out in a tent.

I sat next to the Duchess at tea,
It was just as I feared it would be.
    Her rumblings abdominal
    Were simply phenomenal,
And everyone thought it was me.

There was an old harlot of Wick
  Who was sucking a coal-heaver's prick.
      She said, 'I don't mind
      The coal dust and grime,
But the smell of your balls makes me sick.'

Remember those two of Aberystwyth
  Who connected the things that they pissed with?
      She sat on his lap,
      But they both had the clap,
And they cursed with the things that they kissed with.

A sultan named Abou ben Adhem
  Thus cautioned a travelling madam:
      'I suffer from crabs
      As do most us A-rabs.'
'It's all right,' said the madam, 'I've had 'em.'

There was a young lady of Gaza
Who shaved her cunt clean with a razor.
    The crabs in a lump
    Made tracks to her rump,
Which proceeding did greatly amaze her.

There was a young lady of Michigan
Who said, 'Damn it! I've got the itch again.'
    Said her mother, 'That's strange,
    I'm surprised it ain't mange,
If you've slept with that son-of-a-bitch again.'

Alack, for the doughty O'Connor
Who fucked like a fiend for his honor,
    Till a flapper named Rhea
    Colluded to be a
Mother to Leuco and Gonor.

There was a young man of Back Bay
Who thought syphilis just went away,
    And felt that a chancre
    Was merely a canker
Acquired in lascivious play.

Now first he got acne vulgaris,
The kind that is rampant in Paris.
    It covered his skin,
    From forehead to shin,
And now people ask where his hair is.

With symptoms increasing in number,
His aorta's in need of a plumber,
    His heart is cavorting,
    His wife is aborting,
And now he's acquired a gumma.

Consider his terrible plight –
His eyes won't react to the light,
    His hands are apraxic,
    His gait is ataxic,
He's developing gun-barrel sight.

His passions are strong, as before,
But his penis is flaccid and sore.
      His wife now has tabes
      And sabre-shinned babies –
She's really worse off than a whore.

There are pains in his belly and knees,
His sphincters have gone by degrees.
      Paroxysmal incontinence,
      With all its concomitants,
Brings on unpredictable pees.

Though treated in every known way,
His spirochetes grow day by day.
      He's developed paresis,
      Converses with Jesus,
And thinks he's the Queen of the May.

There was a young girl of Uttoxeter,
And all the young men shook their cocks at her.
From one of these cocks
She contracted the pox,
And she poxed all the cocks in Uttoxeter.

There was a young man of Calcutta
Who tried to write 'Cunt' on a shutter,
He had got to 'C-U-'
When a pious Hindu
Knocked him arse over tit in the gutter.

A marine being sent to Hong Kong
Got his doctor to alter his dong.
He sailed off with a tool
Flat and thin as a rule –
When he got there he found he was wrong.

There was a young man of Madras
  Who was fucking a girl in the grass,
      But the tropical sun
      Spoiled half of his fun
By singeing the hair off his ass.

There was an old rake from Stamboul
  Felt his ardour grow suddenly cool.
      No lack of affection
      Reduced his erection –
But his zipper got caught in his tool.

There was a young lady of Bicester
  Who was nicer by far than her sister:
      The sister would giggle
      And wiggle and jiggle,
But this one would come if you kissed her.

There was a young girl from Hong Kong
Who said, 'You are utterly wrong
    To say my vagina's
    The largest in China,
Just because of your mean little dong.'

There was a young girl of Pitlochry
Who was had by a man in a rockery.
    She said, 'Oh! you've come
    All over my bum,
This isn't a fuck – it's a mockery.'

There was a young girl from Decatur
Who was screwed by an old alligator,
    But nobody knew
    If she relished the screw,
For after he screwed her he ate her.

There was a young lady of Rhyll
In an omnibus was taken ill,
    So she called the conductor,
    Who got in and fucked her,
Which did her more good than a pill.

'My back aches, my penis is sore.
I simply can't fuck any more.
    I'm dripping with sweat,
    And you haven't come yet –
And, my God, it's a quarter to four!'

There was a young girl of Bavaria
Who thought her disease was malaria.
    She went to her doc,
    Who said to her shock,
'It is in the venereal area.'

There was a young lady of Spain
Who took down her pants on a train.
    There was a young porter
    Saw more than he orter,
And asked her to do it again.

In the Garden of Eden lay Adam,
Complacently stroking his madam,
    And loud was his mirth
    For on all of the earth
There were only two balls – and he had 'em.

There was a young lady named Blount
Who had a rectangular cunt.
    She learned for diversion
    Posterior perversion,
Since no one could fit her in front.

There was a young girl name of Sally
Who wanted to dance in the ballet.
  She got roars of applause
  When she kicked off her drawers,
'Cos her hair and her bush didn't tally.

A young man from the banks of the Po
Found his cock had elongated so
  That when he'd pee
  It was not he
But only his neighbours who'd know.

A cautious young fellow named Tunney
Had a whang that was worth any money.
  When eased in half way
  The girl's sigh made him say,
'Why the sigh?' 'For the rest of it, honey.'

There once was a Duchess of Bruges
Whose cunt was incredibly huge.
    Said the King to this dame
    As he thunderously came:
'Mon Dieu! Après moi, le deluge!'

Thank God for the Duchess of Gloucester,
She obliges all who accost her.
    She welcomes the prick
    Of Tom, Harry or Dick,
Or Baldwin or even Lord Astor.

There was a young vampire named Mabel
Whose periods were very unstable.
    One night at full moon
    She took a large spoon
And drank herself under the table.

There was a young fellow named Meek
Who invented a lingual technique.
　　It drove women frantic
　　And made them romantic,
And wore all the hair off his cheek.

A delicate race are the Persians
In the matter of sexual diversions.
　　They co-habit all day,
　　In the usual way,
And the nights are reserved for perversions.

There was a young man from the Falls
Who used to perform in the halls.
　　His favourite trick
　　Was to stand on his prick
And roll off the stage on his balls.

A young lass from near Ballina
Had a bust that would burst any bra.
  She said, 'It's apparent
  That it comes from a parent,
But is it me Ma or me Da?'

A Birmingham virgin antique
Locked a man in her house for a week.
  He entered her door
  With a shout and a roar,
When he left he barely could squeak.

On Mary's fine bosom there leaned
The face of a budding sex fiend,
  But she pulled up his head
  And with sarcasm said,
'Good God, won't you ever be weaned?'

There was a young singer named Springer,
  Got his testicles caught in the wringer.
    He hollered with pain
    As they rolled down the drain,
(falsetto): 'There goes my career as a singer!'

Then up spoke the Bey of Algiers,
  To his harem he shouted, 'My dears,
    You may think it odd of me,
    I've given up sodomy,
Tonight will be fucking.' (Loud cheers.)

There was a young girl of Darjeeling
  Who could dance with such exquisite feeling
    There was never a sound
    For miles around
Save of fly-buttons hitting the ceiling.

There was a young lady named Alice
Who peed in the Vatican Palace.
   It was not dire need
   Made her do this foul deed,
But sheer bloody Protestant malice.

There was a young girl from Cape Cod
Who thought that her child came from God.
   It wasn't the Almighty
   That lifted her nightie,
But Roger, the lodger, the sod.